THE PIANO MUSIC OF
WOLFGANG AMADEUS
MOZART

EIGHT FAVOURITE PIECES

Kevin
Mayhew

We hope you enjoy *The Piano Music of Wolfgang Amadeus Mozart.*
Further copies of this and the other books in the series
are available from your local music shop.

In case of difficulty, please contact the publisher direct:

The Sales Department
KEVIN MAYHEW LTD
Buxhall
Stowmarket
Suffolk IP14 3BW

Phone 01449 737978
Fax 01449 737834
E-mail info@kevinmayhewltd.com

Please ask for our complete catalogue of outstanding Instrumental Music.

First published in Great Britain in 1992 and 1993 by Kevin Mayhew Ltd

This compilation © Copyright 1996 Kevin Mayhew Ltd

ISBN 0 86209 753 3
Catalogue No: 3611189

Cover design by Jonathan Stroulger

Printed and bound in Great Britain

Contents

ANDANTE IN B♭

Wolfgang Amadeus Mozart (1756-1791)

ALLA TURCA from Sonata K.331

Wolfgang Amadeus Mozart (1756-1791)

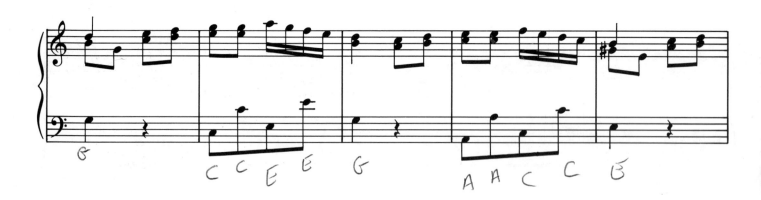

ADAGIO from Sonata K. 570

Wolfgang Amadeus Mozart (1756-1791)

ALLEGRO from Sonata K. 279

Wolfgang Amadeus Mozart (1756-1791)

ANDANTE from Sonata K. 330

Wolfgang Amadeus Mozart (1756-1791)

23

ANDANTINO from Sonata K.311

Wolfgang Amadeus Mozart (1756-1791)

Andantino con espressione

27

ADAGIO IN C

Wolfgang Amadeus Mozart (1756-1791)

RONDO from Sonata K. 545

Wolfgang Amadeus Mozart (1756-1791)